PROFITABLE Baking GUIDE

11 secrets *to* multiply *your* Profit
and run *a* World-Class Bakery

11 secrets *to* multiply *your* Profit
and run *a* World-Class Bakery

AADITYA VIKRAM AGARWAL

Worldwide Publishing by
Pendown Press

PENDOWN PRESS

An ISO 9001 & ISO 14001 Certified Co.,

Regd. Office: 2525/193, 1st Floor, Onkar Nagar-A, Tri Nagar, Delhi-110035

Ph.: 09350849407, 09312235086

E-mail: info@pendownpress.com

Branch Office: 1A/2A, 20, Hari Sadan, Ansari Road, Daryaganj, New Delhi-110002

Ph.: 011-45794768

Website: PendownPress.com

First Edition: 2023

ISBN: 978-93-5554-508-4

Layout and Cover Designed by Pendown Graphics Team

Printed and Bound in India by Thomson Press India Ltd.

The Art of Profitable Baking is hidden
in small nuggets, secrets that can work wonders
for your business if implemented.
Trust me; I talk through my hands-on experience.

TABLE OF CONTENTS

LET'S GET ACQUAINTED!

Hi!

My name is Aaditya Vikram Agarwal.

I am a Modern Bakery Expert. I am a Mechanical Engineer by vocation and a baker by passion.

I am the Technical Director at Nepal's largest, most advanced Flour Mill - RP Agro Industries Pvt Ltd and the Founder-Director of the multiple award-winning, leading Industrial Bakery of Nepal - RP Food & Confectionary Pvt Ltd.

I know this question is coming up right around the corner in your head – Engineer? Baker? How come? - sometimes life has its own plans - it is not what I had thought I would be doing, but I am enjoying it to the core!

I am truly fascinated by all baked products - the process, the versatility, and the infinite possibilities of the number of products that can be baked excite me.

Let me share what I have learnt in my 12 years as a miller & baker - a rare combination which has given me never before insights into the intricacies of this Art.

Over the years, I have used numerous innovations in process & material to continuously build a portfolio of best-selling products. **My experience with all sizes of bakeries - their problems & my solutions has helped them in making a turnaround and even earn healthy profits.**

You must be wondering why I am sharing this insider information with you. I have realised that as owners of bakeries, all of us are sucked into daily operations - that we do not have the time to think outside the box.

People just copy each other and try to compete based on price alone - and that means if someone has a better offer - you lose your sales.

Not just sales, you lose your peace, calm & patience. Customers care about price, but that is not the most significant decision maker – it's the value you offer that changes the game!

Some of the ideas in this book may be known to you, and some may seem trivial or too easy – but that is exactly the point – we don't implement what we know. What is in your mind stays there – it is the action that brings results.

Having gone through the same cycle and succeeded in exiting from this trap - I have learnt 21 things that are sure to boost your profits.

I want to share them with you because I care about you. **My heart wrenches when I hear that someone is not making profits in this industry - and it drives down the value of the entire baking industry of Nepal.**

So, without further ado, **let's make some profits!**

Aaditya Vikram Agarwal
Modern Bakery Expert

Burning Question:

Why are you losing or not making good money when the rest of the industry is making healthy profits?

Despite investing so much effort, time & money in your bakery - what is going wrong? Have you paused to think of this critical question?

Why are some brands hugely successful, while yours not so much, even when your product is better?

Where is the GAP?

I have spoken to umpteen business owners – be it noodle makers, chowmein, biscuit factories, or bakeries, big or small. Size does not matter, and the product can vary, but ultimately, the challenges faced by each one can be narrowed down to 4-6 common problems. They are:

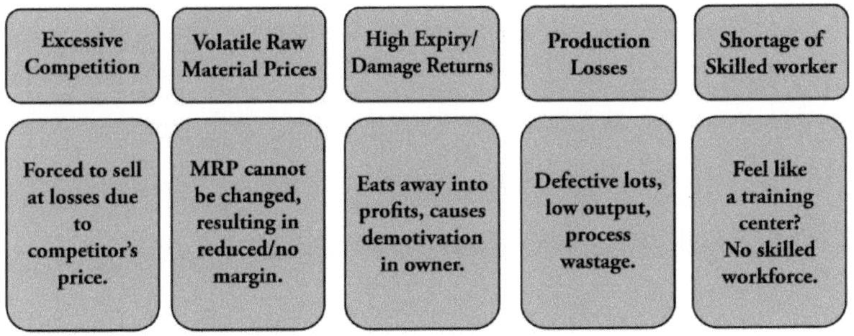

Would you agree that these are the problems? If yes, then if we can address each of them, would your company turn profitable?

However, let me share a very important fact with you – and pay very close attention – **the above challenges are not the problems; they are the symptoms.**

They are the outcome of some decisions taken or not taken by you as an owner. If you merely keep working on these problems, then they will keep coming back. **So, it is important to analyse the root cause and address that.** Once you do, the GAP between losses & profits will close in, become zero, and then you will start making profits.

It really is that simple.

This book is divided into 3 sections.

SECTION 1 is all about understanding the secrets behind choosing the right ingredients and implementing the right techniques of Baking.

SECTION 2 is all about learning and applying the tricks and techniques of the marketing and presentation of the product (s) that you have baked with passion and perfection.

Finally, SECTION 3 is all about hacks and tricks of the trade that will help you stand out head and shoulders above the competition.

Section 1

Cracking The Technique

Chapter 1

THE 7P'S OF FLOUR

For any baked goods, be it cakes, cookies, breads, donuts, pizzas, or brownies, you name it - Flour is the major ingredient. Its percentage share of the end product varies from 25% to even 100% of the final product. Without understanding the parameters of this ingredient, one cannot possibly understand the Art of Baking. Like any other raw material, Flour also has quality measurements which define the performance of that Flour.

In my experience - many bakers are aware of the basic parameters - **moisture, whiteness & gluten.** These are just 3 out of over 50 parameters that define the character of the Flour.

Yes! Over 50! But don't worry, I have got your back - you need not know all of them. I will explain to you the 7 most important parameters in the most simple language so that you will become a power baker yourself.

Let's start with the most popular ones.

1. **Moisture Content** - It basically means how much water content is there in the Flour. So if you hear that the moisture is 15% (which, by the way, is very high), it means that in 1000g of Flour, there is 150gm water. Simple!

2. **Gluten %** - Imagine an elastic rubber balloon. It is stretchable, can hold air, and its size increases when you fill air into it. However, if you overfill it, it will burst & collapse. Some balloons fill easily, some take effort, some grow big, and others burst when blown even a small amount. Similarly, gluten is that part of the Flour which, when combined with water, forms an elastic dough. The higher the gluten %, the higher the strength of the dough network - which means you can stretch it more before it breaks. Lesser gluten means low strength of the dough - which means it will break easily if you stretch it.

3. **Whiteness** - You have seen yellowish flours, silky white flours, and some greyish flours. The color of the Flour depends on many things - mainly on how much Flour has been extracted from the wheat grain. Along with Flour, semolina (suji), wheat flour (atta) and bran (chokar) are also made from the same wheat. The higher the extraction, the darker the Flour. Whole wheat flour (Chakki atta) is, therefore, reddish and dark - because it is almost 100% wheat. Fine quality Bakery flours are, on the other hand, white or creamy - because they are only the innermost, whiter parts of the wheat!

   Now come the ones that matter more.

4. **Water Absorption** - This is a very important aspect that most millers will not share with you. And it has a direct impact on your profits. It is simply how much water you can add to your Flour and still make a good dough and perfect breads. Why is this important? Because water is free of cost.

5. **Ash Content** - It is basically fine impurities that could not be cleaned from the wheat and therefore got milled into Flour. Or it could be the outer layers of wheat (called bran) which have made their way to the final Flour due to improper milling. So what is the impact on the bakery?

   Imagine you have a sharp pin (impurity) in your hand and balloons all around (gluten network, remember the elastic part?). You go around touching those balloons, and they do what? They burst! The dough fails. It's as simple as that - higher ash content means higher impurities in the Flour, which act like blades - they will break the gluten network and make the dough weak.

6. **Particle Size** - As the name says - when you take the Flour between your fingers, do you feel silky textured Flour with no scratching? That is fine Flour with small particle sizes. Instead, if you can feel some particles, grainy or powdery like fine sand, that is a thick flour with large particle sizes.

7. **Extraction %** - Extraction % indicates how much Flour has been milled from 1000g of wheat. If only 500g, then extraction is 50%. If the flour company has milled 750g flour out of 1000g, then extraction is 75%. This has a big impact on the baking quality. I will explain this point further in the coming pages.

   These are the most basic quality parameters that you need to know to start on your way to successful Baking.

Chapter 2

HOW TO SELECT THE RIGHT FLOUR?

Breads need to rise. Cakes dream to crumble in your mouth. Cookies are made to spread & crack. Donuts need to be soft & spongy. Momos are obsessed with being skinny. While Pizzas want to have an airy crust. Noodles spend all the time admiring their long, slender strands, While Khari is busy puffing about its day!

One of the most important secrets to making profits in the bakery business comes down to this - selecting the right Flour.

In the last chapter, I told you about the only 7 parameters that matter. These should be your 7 talking points with a flour supplier. Not the price.

Let us say you want to purchase a car. You have a specific budget in mind, and you go to the showrooms of all the leading brands and ask for many specs such as engine power, mileage, tyre size, number of seats, safety features etc. After much thought, you finalise the best model based on the price and drive back home with it. But, when you try to park it in your garage, you find that the car is bigger than the length of the garage!

Your car does d not fit in your garage. It is not the right car for you, and there is a mismatch.

There are 2 takeaways from this story - first that you should know what those 7 parameters are in the Flour that you are buying.

Second, you need to know what parameter is right for the product that you want to bake. This is the reason why most bakeries face issues like the following:

1. Variation in product quality.
2. Failed mixes - leading to huge loss of raw material & labour costs.
3. Various faults in baking.
4. Low output of end product - leading to lost profit.
5. Unattractive products - leading to lost brand value and disappointed customers.

I want you to absorb this fact once & for all: One size does not fit all.

It is critical to know the ideal values of the 7P's depending on the product that you want to make.

Now, I have come across multiple cases where bakers ask for Flour with high gluten content. And then they try to bake high-quality cakes with it but are disappointed that it does not perform! You do not need high gluten content for cakes in most cases - it is bad for the recipe!

On the other hand, if he were baking bread - then high gluten content would be a necessity. Do you see the point? The baker must be absolutely clear as to what he wants to bake.

A flour that performs well in cookies will absolutely wreck the bread dough. A flour that makes perfect noodles will cause havoc in the cakes.

So, what can be done about it?

In the table below, I have listed the ideal values of the parameters based on the product you want to bake.

Product	Gluten	Ash Content	Particle Size	Extraction %	Water Absorption
Bread/ Buns	11-14%	max 0.60	fine	50-60%	high
Cookies	7-9%	0.65-0.80	medium	65-70%	low
Puff	8-9%	0.60-0.65	medium	60-65%	moderate
Cakes	7-8%	max 0.55	very fine	45-55%	low
Rusk	10-12%	max 0.60	medium	50-60%	moderate
Pizza	11-13%	0.50-0.55	fine	50-55%	low

Armed with this table, you are closer to your journey to becoming a profitable baker.

The next time that you purchase Flour keep in mind to ask your supplier for these parameters to your supplier - and you will be surprised. While 2-3 parameters may be addressed, you are most likely to receive a blank answer regarding most of the others.

Speciality Flours

With so much new insight, you must be wondering - all this is fine - but there is only one type of Flour available in the market. And it is not possible to remember each parameter each time a baker buys a bag of Flour.

What to do??

Worry not.

Each of the most suitable flours has a name. Let me list them out for you.

All Purpose Flour - As the name says - it is a general flour with all values of the parameters as an average - nothing is too much or too less, and it will generally make all the baked goods of satisfactory quality. It is the jack of all trades. If you want to keep things simple and have too many varieties of products with low quantities - then you can use this Flour.

Baker's (Bread) Special Flour - Now, this is a special flour for bakers - and the specifications and end use can vary from company to company, but generally, these flours are best for breads or any yeast-raised products - with high gluten content, low ash, finely milled and low extraction %. They rise well and are able to absorb more water than AP flours, and if you want to have the best output (read high profits) from breads - then this is the Flour to go for.

Cake SP Flour - Cakes need to be crumbly and soft, and they should not taste like bread - so it needs a different flour as well. These are very finely milled and have low gluten & very low ash content so that the crumb appears attractive. Cakes made from this Flour are soft, will melt in the mouth and just blow your customer away.

I will let you in on another big secret of the flour milling industry related to Extraction %. There are majorly 4 products that a flour miller makes from wheat in varying ranges -

1. Flour (Maida): 40 to 70%
2. Atta: 5 to 30%
3. Semolina (Suji) : 2-5%
4. Wheat Bran (Chokar) - 25 to 30%

If you see the minimum and maximum ranges, you will see that the total goes above 100%. This means that if a normal flour mill that is not making speciality flour for the industry has a higher demand for atta, then the Extraction % of atta is increased to 30%, and the flour extraction is reduced to 40%. Similarly, in the opposite case, flour extraction is increased to 65%, and atta extraction is reduced to a mere 5%.

And there is no difference in the Flour with 40% extraction vs 65% extraction for most commercial millers - they pack it in the same bag. So, when you bought the 1st Flour, you got 40% flour, and the second time, the same-looking bag contained 65% Extraction flour.

Now, if the Purchase Manager has set their parameters as per the 65% flour, then the 40% flour will also pass the parameters with flying colours - as it is a better flour. BUT, when the head baker mixes these 2 flours for the same bread - he will get vastly different results - this means that all the settings on the machines - the mixing time, the formulation, the behaviour of the dough in the divider and moulder will have to be modified. This only results in confusion, irritation and loss.

How do you solve this?

This is only solvable by buying from millers who have the capabilities to make speciality flours - because they have FIXED THEIR FLOUR RECIPES! A speciality flour means that not only the 7Ps but all the other technical parameters have been maintained within a range.

Ask your supplier this question - have you fixed your flour recipe? Can they give you absolutely the same Flour on Day 365 as on Day 1?

Chapter 3

BUYING RIGHT

The rule is very simple – but one that we forget each time we buy ourselves or ask our Purchase Manager to buy on our behalf.

Most of us operate from the mindset of *mehanga ho gaya, sasta do* (this is too expensive, give me the cheaper one).

On the other hand, there are some of us who say *sabse accha quality ka chahiye* (give me the best quality that you have).

So, the procurement of raw materials is either based on the price or quality of the raw material in question.

Whereas the real question should be this – Is this the right material for the product that I want to sell? The decision must come from what you want to make, whom you want to sell to and what the customer expects.

You can buy the highest quality raw materials and make world-class products – but if you are in a village where buying power is weak – it will not sell!

On the other hand, if you take the cheapest available raw material and try to sell low-quality products in a premium market, customers will not buy it either!

To make my point clearer, I would like to illustrate it with a small story:

Binod Bhattarai had just returned to Nepal from Dubai after a 5-year long work experience in a leading bakery.

He was excited as he dreamt of owning his own bakery in his hometown of Surkhet and now had learnt all the skills of making the best-baked delicacies under an expert chef.

After investing his savings in a world-class setup, he set out to find the Flour, butter, baking powders and other ingredients. However, he was in for a shock.

He was utterly confused! He wanted a strong flour for bread and a weak flour for cakes, but his neighbourhood supplier had just Flour– he had no idea whether it was weak or strong!

Obviously, he did not have the budget or the skill to set up a lab for every ingredient – that data should have been available to him from the manufacturer.

Without knowing the properties of his raw materials, how could he make different varieties of bread or cakes?

So, the question is – how to find the right material?

Ans.: Find the Right Supplier.

The Right Supplier

Professional-grade raw materials are found with a few suppliers – and there are a few things to look out for before finalising one.

- Timely delivery @ smaller quantities - because it means lesser investment in working capital, lower space requirement & no loss due to expiry of old stock.
- All-time availability of stock
- Should be technically competent
- Should be able to provide customer support
- Help you in innovating

The Right Professional Grade Product

Professional-grade raw materials are not available in the general marketplace. They are called professional-grade because they are specially prepared for industrial use. Here is why they are critical to building your profits:

1. Higher Yield means higher profit.
2. Consistent performance regardless of the weather
3. Specialised as per product, better finish & quality
4. Critical for innovation.

I totally understand the natural human behaviour to buy the cheapest available raw material and get the best bargain - it is necessary. After all, money saved is money earned. However, we often only think about the up-front cost instead of the actual cost of return.

For e.g., a general yeast would take 2.5 hours to proof at a dosage of 2%. Whereas a professional yeast will only take 2 hours at a lower dose of 1.5%! You save much more even though the professional grade yeast is 5-10% more expensive than general yeast.

Another way to calculate is this:

The total raw material cost per kg in any recipe should be less than the selling price of the product to be able to make a profit. Right?

Say flour costs around NPR 70/- per kg at the time of writing this book. While bread's average selling price is about NPR 170/- per kg. A Professional flour may cost NPR 72/- per Kg. However, if one 50 kg bag of Flour gives you even one more kg of bread output, it means you save an additional NPR 70/- for each bag of Flour (NPR 170- (50kg x NPR 2/-) paid extra).

Chapter 4

IS BAKING A GAME OF LUCK FOR YOU?

Sometimes it bakes great - but sometimes, it completely fails or is not satisfactory.

This is a common concern that I have heard from many of my interactions with bakers as a Modern Bakery Expert.

This is where the Art of Baking shows its true meaning - that it is an art with a science behind it. While there can be a plethora of reasons for this variation in quality ranging from changes in temperature, changes in humidity, different mixing times, wrong baking temperatures, process faults, and defective raw materials - for the sake of simplicity, I will assume that you have the basics right.

From my experience, in 75% of the cases, when bakeries have their processes under control, the culprit for variation in quality can be attributed to variation in the quality of the Flour. What does this mean?

For consistent results, consistent quality of Flour is a must.

Temperature

A basic rule that most bakers know but very few follow is that we must maintain dough temperature at all costs. All you need is a thermometer with a probe/needle that you can stick inside the material/dough to instantly tell you the temperature. It does not cost more than a few hundred rupees and will pay for itself in less than a day's time.

Why is this important? Because, my dear reader, your recipe most likely contains a living organism - yeast. Yes, it is alive! Millions of tiny bacteria that are waiting for sugar, water and warmth to start producing carbon dioxide (CO2)- the gas that causes bread to rise. It is just like us humans - we freeze and cannot do much activity in sub-zero temperatures, and neither can we tolerate the scorching heat of the deserts. But you can see all of us jumping up and down on the beach with full energy on a perfectly warm summer afternoon, sipping a glass of chilled cola (or beer)!

Similarly, yeast cells also thrive and produce maximum CO2 when they are given ample sugar, water and temperatures between 28 to 35 deg C.

While most of the powder ingredients, such as Flour, sugar, oils, fat, yeast etc., are likely to be stored at room temperature, you can control the final dough temperature by adding ice or cold water. However, this should be a guessing game left to approximation. There is a very simple calculation by which you can determine exactly how much ice or cold water needs to be added.

For your benefit, I am going to give you another gift. You can use this link: https://bit.ly/DoughTemp_Aaditya to download an excel table where you enter the values taken with your thermometer, and the table will tell you exactly how much ice and water is required to reach the desired dough temperature (DDT) of 27-28 deg C after mixing.

If the dough reaches this DDT, then it will gain about 5-7 deg C during moulding and panning, and an ideal temperature of 35-36 deg C will be achieved for proofing.

Weighing & Measurements

The biggest difference between modern bakeries and local ones is that they stick to accurate measurements of each item. It can be a bulk ingredient, such as Flour and sugar, or a minor ingredient, such as salt. During my visits and observations of many small-scale industries, I watched with awe as the head chef simply "sprinkled" salt in the mixer bowl without measurement!

To become a brand, you have to be able to promise consistency. To avoid losses due to defective lots, you have to ensure accurate weighing and measurements. Each & every item that goes into that bowl must be weighed. There can be a tolerance, but that tolerance is not measured in grams.

Allow me to illustrate my point. If a recipe demands 50 kg of Flour and the chef adds 50.050 Kg (50 gms more than prescribed), then it is fine. But if the recipe demands 400 gm salt, and the chef adds 450g (50g more), then the result will be entirely different!

So tolerances have to be defined in % and not in absolute values. On a smaller scale of operations, a 1-1.5% tolerance is acceptable. Depending on your skill level, this variance should be as low as possible.

Timing & Process

With the temperature and measurements taken care of, the next important factor is timing and process. This is one place where I have seen even bigger bakeries and factories falter.

From mixing to time on the table to proving and then to Baking. Then cooling, slicing and packing. Each stage should be controlled with time. The conditions and processes followed by each one may differ - so there cannot be one standard time defined for everyone. That is for you to observe - how much time does my bread take to proof? How much time does it cool sufficiently so that I can slice it without any damage? Even within your bakery - where you keep it will affect the cooling time - keep it near the window, and it cools faster. If you keep the baked goods near the oven, it dries out and takes longer.

So the key takeaway is - define your process and note the timings in your own unit. Then follow it no matter what. Make adjustments for season and weather, change in ingredients, but take charge. Be in control of what goes on.

Chapter 5

THE MAGIC OF WATER ABSORPTION

I have explained the importance of one of the 7P's - Water Absorption in the very beginning. Here, I want to reiterate the importance of this factor with a more practical yet simple calculation.

1. **Type 1:** You are adding, let us say, 25kg water to 50 kg flour = 75kg dough (khameer). You then divide them into 400g pieces yielding approximately 188 breads after Baking. Assuming a selling price of 40/- per bread, the total product is worth Rs.7520/-
2. **Type 2:** You are able to add 30kg water to 50Kgs = 80 Kg dough of this Type 2 flour, and still, the dough is workable. You divide them again into 400g pieces - but this time, you get 200 breads of the same quality as before. Now the breads are worth 8000/-!

From where did these extra 12 breads come? The second Professional Flour was able to add a full Rs. 480/- for 1 bag of 50 kg flour to your profit without any extra cost! For Free! Imagine doing this over and over again for the entire year!

The Magic lies in Water Absorption - That is the hidden Profit of Baking.

Section 2

Smart Selling & Magnetic Marketing

Chapter 6

WHAT LOOKS GOOD, SELLS MORE

When it comes to food, it is said that you consume the dish with your eyes before you eat it. What it means is if your product is good looking, attractive, mouth-watering, clean, and baked to a beautiful golden color then the customer who is holding that packet in their hand is already convinced to buy it.

Let us look at a few pictures. Why don't you choose which product you will buy if you had an option between:

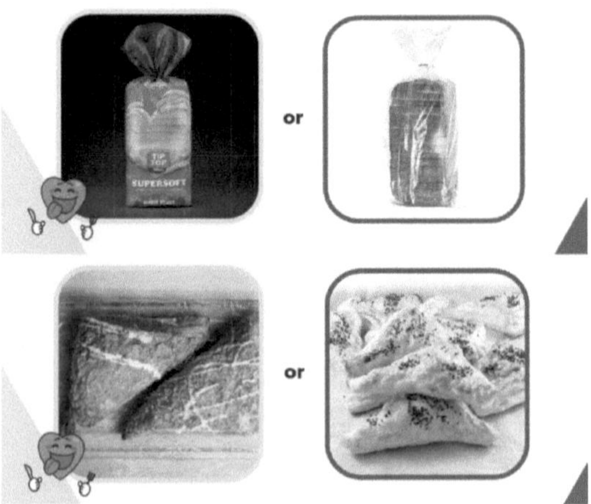

I am 100% sure your heart would have fluttered for the products on the left, without exception, in each case.

That is the power & importance of looks and presentation. However, in many cases, we, as entrepreneurs, and bakery owners, are very caught up with all the other operational roles that we don't pay enough attention to the branding, packaging, looks & feel of the product.

Remember, the customers see only the finished product! They decide whether to buy or not based on only what their eyes see. It does not matter to the buyer if you were awake till 2 am in the morning engrossed in accounts or out in the market to purchase raw materials yourself.

If what comes out of the oven does not look good, it will either not sell, or you will have to sell just like everyone else – cheap.

So, how can you decide whether your product fits the criteria of "looking awesome"?

I have prepared a simple, doable 7 **Point "I Look Awesome"** Checklist that I share with you below out of pure care. I have used this for each of the products that we have launched in the last 10 years, and not once has this checklist failed me! So, here it is:

Checkpoint	Box	Remedy (If the box is not ticked)
Does the pack/ product have a brand name? If yes, is it the biggest thing visible on the pack?		Think of a unique brand name. Get it registered with the government to avoid legal conflicts as well as prevent duplicacy. The brand name can be different from the registered name of your business.
Most baked items/ noodles sold fresh are sold in open format or in transparent packs. If so, is the color golden brown? Are the colors of all the packets of the same item similar, or is there variation?		Check if you are overbaking/ underbaking. If the variation is there between packs, check the oven's setting- is the heat being distributed evenly?
If it is an open item (e.g. Pastry) – don't call it Chocolate Pastry – think of a unique name and place a tag with your brand's logo on the shelf.		Think of names that can stand out. Anyone can copy a recipe, but the first to name their product uniquely sits in the buyer's mind.

Is the product clean and free from oil spots, burnt particles, and black deposits.		Schedule cleaning of your utensils every week. Keep 3-4 hours every week for cleaning only. You may feel it costs money, but remember, a dirty product will shut down your business!
Is the packing material of high clarity?		Cheaper, dull-quality poly, such as LD or HM, may save cost. But clear shiny materials such as BOPP and CPP will make the packet much more attractive.
For retail bakeries, is your counter clean? No hand marks, no blurred lines, and lots of lighting are a must.		An attractive, well-lit, clean & clear glass shelf is the biggest asset of a retail bakery. Clean it thrice a day (yes, or more) with old newspapers & a spray of Colin for a stellar shine!
Clearly printed date, MRP & Batch coding.		A printed tag or print on the pack builds trust in the customer's mind.

Chapter 7

INCREASE CUSTOMER FLOW

mera accha mera accha nai..mera accha...

saari bheed yaha par...kyon?

I am sure you have all been to a busy marketplace. It is very common to see a sight like the one shown above – many shopkeepers are in the same area, selling almost the same thing, yet all the customers are flocking to one store. Everyone is saying, "buy from me, I have good stuff", welcoming you to their store, but no one can match the customer flow of that one main shop.

Even in the case of bakeries, the case is similar. So, how can you stand out from the rest? How can you attract customers like bees are to honey?

There are several simple, immediately doable strategies.

1. **Taste-Like-Buy:** We underestimate the power of free sampling. We think that if we give customers free tasting – we will run into losses, and people will taste but will not buy. However, that is not the case. Look at the photographs shared below closely:

taste - like - BUY!

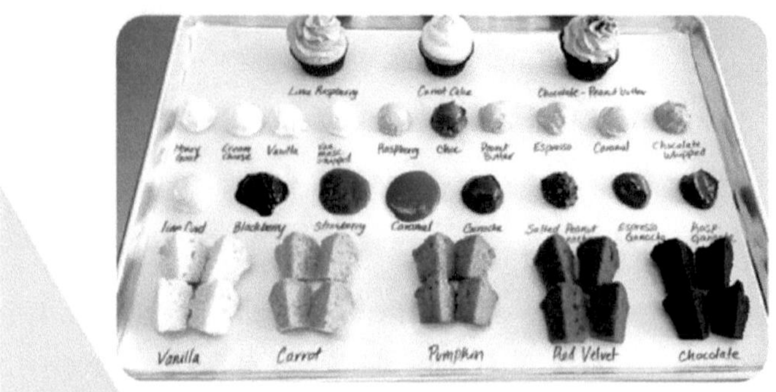

People will never buy from your outlet if they are already addicted to another. The only chance you have of converting them to your customers is to get them to taste your product – once – anyhow – even for free.

By not doing so, you are losing a customer for life.

I ask you, how much will one small piece of cake cost? Can you not divide a muffin into four small pieces? **It will cost peanuts! And customers will love it.**

You do not have to do it all day long. Timing is crucial. Do it in the evenings, when people are returning from the office so that the husband or wife can take them home for their family. Do it when the school bell rings for the day so that the children can taste it and crave for it the next day.

Set a cap for yourself – say 5% of your total targeted sales per day for sampling.

Bigger, more successful companies keep up to 10-15% for this. But for a start, try 5%, and then when you see that more customers are coming to the store, increase the % even higher for better results. That will also create a limited time frame mentality, and customers will visit your store before any other.

Before moving on to the next step, I want to ask you – will you implement this from tomorrow? If you have any doubts, please shelf them. Try it once. No harm in doing so.

2. **Your Gold Mine Database:** It is one of the most powerful yet most ignored tools. 95% of the local bakeries do not maintain a database of their customers. The top 5%, on the other hand, know their customers so well that the moment they send out a marketing message or call, they bring in lakhs of rupees in sales.

So how to do it? It is very simple., I am giving you this very powerful Gold Mine Database format as a gift. You can type it on the computer, or maintain it in a diary, wherever you are comfortable.

The Gold Mine Database

Buyer's Name	Bought for	Occasion	Date of Occasion	Address	Contact Number	Email Id	Ordered
Binod	Wife	Anniversary	20Th Sep 2010	Surkhet	Xxx992991	sasdf@ gmail.com	½ lb Black forest, custom.
Deepa	Brother	Birthday	21st Sep 1990	Jumla	Xxx8391929	add@mail. com	3 lb Pineapple, Ferrari Car

Now comes the question, if we have this data for each customer who enters the shop, what can we do with it?

Almost everyone uses a smartphone today. Most of your potential customers are on social media, use email and communicate with them using Viber, Whatsapp, Telegram, Messenger, and the like.

The above format is called "Gold Mine" for a reason – if used properly, you can literally be sure that every time you communicate the right message to your database, it will respond with a jump in sales.

For, e.g., you can call Binod from the above table on 15th September in the coming year and offer him a special discount on a customised Black Forest Anniversary cake for his wife, due on the 20th of September. He will remember it for life, and not to say if he had forgotten, he will thank you from his heart! Isn't that sweet?

How about sending a WhatsApp message to Deepa with a photograph of the latest Ferrari customised cake 3 days before her brother's birthday & even throwing in a toy car as a gift from your end?

If this is not true care for your customers, then what is? If you can do this, the customers will be so delighted that, most likely, they will not bargain for price with you – because you are delivering them much more value than they ever expected!

3. **Change the Equation:** They say what got you here will not get you where you want to be.

It is a profound statement. It means that to change the direction of your business, earn more profit, lean away from price wars, avoid customer ***chik-chik*** and grow, you must change the way you have worked till now.

How to do it?

I will break it up into four very easy lines of thought so that you can examine each one in your current business and apply whatever you feel works for you.

To change the equation, you can basically change any or all of the following:

Any changes, be they incremental or revolutionary, in these quadrants will directly impact your business's future.

Let me give you a few examples so that you can understand this important aspect in a better way.

Product

Let us say you have a retail bakery outlet with your main product as occasion cakes & pastries. However, there are at least 10 other similar outlets that you must compete with within your area. What can you do to your product that is different from the market? Can you innovate new flavours or a new form of packaging? Can you add 3 new types of brownies or start serving coffee and cookies as well so that customers can spend some time in your shop and try other products as well?

Delivery

How are your customers buying from you? Do they visit your shop to place orders? Do you show them a photograph of what they will get? Can they place orders over the phone? Or do you have a web application on which customers can place their orders? Can you arrange for delivery at their address? Do you offer late-night deliveries?

What can you change in your delivery method so that the customer gets more value and feels it is easier to buy from you than others?

Customer or Market: If you think you can run one bakery to serve all types of customers, you are wrong. **You may be able to, but you will never attain cult status.** That can only come with focus. That is because each type of customer has different needs, preferences and purchasing power. In our earlier example, if Binod were to make and serve premium chocolate-filled croissants from his outlet in a small village, they would hardly sell. So, it is important to define the customer you are targeting. Trying to be the jack of all traders will mean you are the master of none. And you cannot command the best profits and brand in your bakery if you are not recognised as a master of something.

Marketing

Out of the four things that can be changed, the most crucial, implementable and high-impact change that you can bring about is in marketing. It is also the easiest to execute.

I will first give you a very simple and easy-to-understand definition of marketing. Hold on before you judge – it is different from what you have heard till now. I learnt this from my mentor Akshar Yadav, a top-notch marketing guru:

> '**Marketing** *is presenting your* **product or service** *to* **your potential customers** *in* **such a way** *that makes them eager to buy."*
>
> **~Akshar Yadav**

Read it again and again. At least 5 times, and absorb every word.

We, as human beings, enjoy buying but do not enjoy being sold to. **There is a very thin line, but the difference determines whether the customer sees you as a pushy, desperate salesman or a reliable authority figure.**

What can you say and show to **only** your potential customers – be it over the phone, face to face, in a radio ad, or on a Facebook post that will make them say, "Wow, this is exactly what I was looking for!"

Section 3

The Keys to a Profitable Bakery Business

Chapter 8

REDUCE EXPIRY & RETURNS

The single biggest leakage of profits.

Every hardworking baker goes through this traumatising experience. Waking up at 5 am to put the first batch of bread in the proofer while the sun is just about to show up. The team toils hard to bake batch after batch of perfect bread. The salesperson delivers it to individual shops, and one would assume that the job is done. The bread is sold, and the profits have been booked.

Alas, only if it were so easy! How many of you have had to witness a huge amount of those breads being returned to you after 4-6 days because they went unsold at the shop?

I do not speak for everyone, but in competitive markets like Nepal and India, it is a standard practice that whatever the shopkeeper is unable to sell will be taken back by the manufacturer in case it expires on the shelf!

Here, the generally accepted and calculated expiry returns are estimated to be around 1.15 to 2.00% and this cost is factored in by any baker in determining the selling price.

However, I have witnessed returns as high as 34%. Yes, you read correctly – a whopping 34%! I have seen the bakery owner's eyes water up when each delivery van after van unloaded the unsold breads.

The question to ask is: **Is there a way to plug this leak?** Is there a way to stop yourself from burnout?

It is difficult to change the dynamics of the market immediately – then what can you do about it?

Step 1: First, change your mindset. Believe that the impact due to the policy of accepting returns can be minimised. Question the status quo. Open your mind to new possibilities. Here's how:

Step 2: In most cases, the sales team or the retail baker is aware of the number of days that have gone by with the product sitting unsold. Instruct them to collect the unsold goods 2 days before the expiry date. I am assuming here that a packet of bread lasts for 5-6 days before it goes stale. Remember, if it has not sold in 2 days, it is even more unlikely that it will sell now – because other competitors and you as well have already supplied newer, fresher, softer bread to the same shop.

Most customers always pick up the bread, press-test it for softness, check the date and want the newest one.

Step 3: What do you do with these baked items which still have life in them? **You can do quite a lot to minimise the loss.** Remember, I am only giving you a few guidelines to open your mind to the possibility – you will need to understand and tweak these ideas for your own use.

Now, outside your bakery or shop, put up a table with the sign "**Bread for Half-price after 06. 00 pm**". Sell the short-date breads at half price to the customers who come only to your bakery. You may be screaming inside – if I do this, then no one will buy my fresh bread from the market! Take a step back and see – you will find it only to be your assumption.

Not everyone will take you up on the half-price offer. Who will? Maybe some bulk consumers – a caterer who has a conference that evening, a marriage party, or some social event. The caterer or the restaurant knows that they are getting good to serve bread at a price no one else will give him. They might even say to you – I will buy all of it!

Another opportunity could be to test out a new product that you are trying out. Put up a board "Free Bread with purchase of Newly launched Chocochip Muffins".

The new product will reach your target audience immediately, and you can bundle the still-fresh bread as an irresistible offer.

The possibilities are many – you must believe that this scenario is in your control – that you can do something about it rather than sitting on the sidelines and watching while your profit leaks uncontrollably.

Chapter 9

INNOVATE PROFITABLE PRODUCTS

Innovation

Innovation is where the sales and margins live. I recommend to each baker that I meet – do not copy. Innovate. There is the possibility of infinite new products that you can mix, match, try and make.

The customer has endless options – how do you stand out in his/her eyes?

For e.g. What do you notice about the stack of chips below:

This is what most packets of chips look like – and they taste similar. They are mostly priced between Rs. 10 to Rs. 50 per pack, and there is a fierce price war in this segment.

However, this box of Pringles stands out – because of innovation in shape and packaging. There is hardly any competition since the customer cannot compare with any other packet of chips, and they are willing to pay 4-5 times the price!

That is the power of innovation.

Let me show you another example:

Why is it that amongst the hundreds of varieties of chocolate-flavoured biscuits, Oreo was able to innovate with its offering of dark chocolate biscuits with vanilla cream and position it with milk?

Another example would be a regular stack of wheat flour (maida) compared to a range of high-performance application-based speciality flour:

My point is innovation is what makes you stand apart from the competition – it is a big word per se, but you can do it. Start by innovating small – try out a new cream flavour in the next black forest cake that you bake. Innovate in the shape or size of the cookie. Make a small batch of sourdough or rich butter bread.

Each time you innovate, you move ahead of the competition – especially in the eyes of the customer.

To be able to innovate, you must have a skilled team – who, with the right training, knowledge and experience, can propel your bakery to the next level of expansion – 400% growth!

By using the below 5-step method, you can innovate like a pro:

1. Identify the Gap in your Portfolio & choose a product you want to create.
2. Search for suitable recipes. You can scour the internet for inspiration and then tweak the recipes to your liking.
3. Procure the right ingredients for the same and make a small batch.
4. Conduct a trial tasting round for your best customers and log their feedback.
5. Go back to Step 4 to refine the recipe as per feedback.
6. Connect to your Database and let them know that you are launching a new product. Invite them for free sampling.

Chapter 10

MONEY LYING ON THE FLOOR

Imagine that you have been running your bakery for some time now. Slowly and steadily, as the equipment becomes old, they develop tolerances & gaps.

You have your hard-earned money invested in the raw material, and a skilled, expensive baker mixes those ingredients. In my many years of hands-on experience, I have seen small, repeating wastages at every stage of the process. Some of the dough is left behind in the mixer. On the moulding table, the dough reaches the end and some falls to the ground. There is leakage in the machine's hopper, and with each stroke of the depositor, some dough gets pushed out from the sides.

You can see a few pictures of the same.

Remember, this is not dough; this is the end product wasted. It is money wasted! Spend 1 day per week in your bakery with your eyes only on this - where all the dough, baked goods or in-process material has fallen on the ground or is leaking. Find out the source and how it can be plugged in. This alone will save you a huge sum of money.

I will share a small story - When I did this exercise for the first time in my own bakery, you will be surprised to know that the total weight of the wasted material was 35 Kg, and we were producing 700 Kg of finished goods at that point. It means a huge 5% wastage! Spending time to locate these wastages and solve the problems alone increased our profit by the value of 35 Kg!

Further, I want to tell you another secret - **Keep repeating this exercise every week, and you will see that when you start plugging these wastages, in a few weeks, your wastage % will keep getting smaller, and your profit will keep shooting up!**

Take out time for this - because while you are busy selling, buying, making, and running on your toes, you are losing money through a hole in your pocket.

Chapter 11

FIX YOUR RECIPE

I will illustrate this point with a very simple example.

Just 1 question - does your morning tea taste the same every day?

Sometimes it is boiled just right, the quantity of tea leaves & its combination with milk and water is just what you need, and you enjoy it. Sometimes it is not so good, and on a few occasions, it's so bad you have to throw it away! But since this is happening in your own kitchen, you are forgiving in nature and don't fire the cook (and cannot even think of firing your significant other) over this.

Do you see the point?

I have visited over 100 bakeries in our country over the past 12 years - and was surprised to see that very few were actually fixing their recipes! By fixing your recipe - I do not mean just following a formulation. It's much deeper than that!

Let us say you launched a chocolate chip cookie - it is a hit instantly, and you have customers queuing up outside your bakery to buy the same. What a lovely cookie! Suddenly, your Choco chip cookie fan lovers start complaining to you that the taste is not as good as before, and you start losing sales.

What went wrong? You have not changed the recipe. On digging further, you found that the cocoa powder that you had been using since the beginning was not available, and your head baker decided to purchase the same profile powder from another manufacturer. Bang! There goes your product, and your most loyal customers walk away from you.

Similarly, each of the ingredients that go into your product needs to be fixed - do not change the brand, quantity, flavour or type of ingredient that goes into the recipe. If it works, keep it the same. If people love it, then they want the same taste each time. The same look, the same feel, the same authenticity each time they eat it. Any variations will mean a loss of your reputation.

RECAP

With this, I reach the end of my book. To summarise what I have shared, here's everything at a scannable glance:

- I covered the **technical parameters of Flour,** its importance in Baking and its impact on the quality of the final product.
- Then I included a mini-guide on **how to select the right type of raw material** and introduced the concept of **Professional Grade material.** I also touched briefly upon what you should look for in finalising the **Right Supplier** for your industry.
- Having taken care of that, I shared a few **conditions to take care of so that Baking is not like a game of luck** for you.
- In Section 2, I introduced **very usable, immediately applicable strategies on branding,** the importance of maintaining **your own Database** and how to increase customer flow.
- From there, in Section 3, I shared **some must-know key profitability factors** were written - like how to **reduce expiry returns** and how **innovation** will help you in the next round of super-growth.

- I have also spoken about a largely ignored loss maker - process waste. Last but not least, I reiterated the criticality of fixing your recipe.

To be honest, there could be 11 separate books written about each of these 11 strategies. However, I have ensured that all the key details are available to you in 1 book that is easy to absorb and implement.

This book will serve as a ready reference guide that you can use at every step of your process. From here, you can pick up any strategy you think will help you the most and **implement it for guaranteed success.**

IMPLEMENTATION IS THE KEY

Dear Baker, Now you have 2 choices.

You can keep this book as your profitable baking bible - and try to solve all the issues you are having on your own. I know you will succeed, but chances are that the next phone call from a customer will take your attention away, or you will be sucked back into operations.

Or

You can have me, Aaditya Vikram Agarwal, a Modern Bakery Expert, by your side to help you achieve all these.

You may email me at aaditya@rpgroupnepal.com if you get stuck anywhere or require further understanding of the subject. You can also reach out to me if you are a fellow baker and want to share any feedback and insights on the book.

I receive 100s of emails every day and write back to each one of them. Because I also have my own businesses to look after, there might be a little delay due to our bookings, but I assure you that you will receive a quick response.

9 789355 545084

Printed by Libri Plureos GmbH in Hamburg, Germany